PUMPKIN SPICE FOR YOUR SOUL

25 Devotions for Autumn

by Anna E. Rendell

ISBN: 978-1-946195-26-5

Cover art and design by Jennifer Tucker, littlehousestudio.net.
Interior design by Jared Rendell, jaredrendell.com
Edited by Peggy Johnson and Mary Carver
Author photo on back cover by Jennifer Faris, jenniferfaris.com

Printed in the United States of America.

AnnaRendell.com

Dedicated to those who wait all the year for autumn –
especially to my sister, Amy,
who has always been one such soul.

TABLE OF CONTENTS

EXTRAS:

INTRODUCTION

The colors of autumn. From early sunrises pink and purple to evening sunsets streaking red and orange. The rusty orange of pumpkins ripe and waiting on vines of leafy green. Warm and golden-hued September flows into yellow-orange and cool October, which gives way to the brisk air and deep reds of November.

Roasted root vegetables in carroty orange, butternut yellow, fragrant purple onion, creamy cauliflower, and potato peel brown. Mottled orange pumpkins on porches and in kitchens, ready to turn into bread and pie, cheesecake and soup. Squash of every tone. Kale in dark green and dusky purple. Bright red Honeycrisp apples hanging off vibrant green trees. Shiny green Granny Smiths plucked, then covered in golden caramel. A red and green bowlful of apples, waiting to be sliced into white crescents and dotted with gingery red cinnamon spice, ready to bake into an apple crisp.

Yellow buses hitting the road after their summer vacation. Dark red brick school buildings filled once again with faces of all colors, raising flags up silver poles that unfurl against brilliant blue sky. Golden wheat stalks and leafy green corn husks displayed by the acre. Rich black soil flecked with earthworms, and brown acorns and pinecones falling from trees that are turning inward. Freshly painted white lines on a green football field, ready to catch quarterbacks and guide marching bands.

Pumpkin spice lattes – coffee brown in a white paper cup, a hint of ginger around the edges, and whipped cream sprinkled with fragrant nutmeg.

Is there anything more beautiful than the colors – and tastes – of autumn? Beauty, glory, divine touches around every corner. It's a wonder we get anything done all season. I, for one, only want to curl up with a good book and a hot pumpkin spice latte, tucked into a cozy little corner of my porch, fireplace blazing while leaves lazily drift to the ground, and my kids wearing the first sweatshirts of the season while playing in piles of fallen leaves. Isn't that the most idyllic picture of fall, and the one we hold onto all year?

Too bad that scene occurs about one time during the whole season and lasts all of three minutes. It's especially "too bad" when my frayed edges crave smoothing – my soul crying for the beauty of autumn, the coziness of a steaming pumpkin spice latte, and a moment in that comfy chair.

But what if we leaned in deeply to that one occurrence? Better yet, what if that kind of moment could happen more than once a season?

Autumn is the perfect time to take back the reins of our self-care intentions. To pause and actually care for ourselves. Let's enjoy our lattes, oh yes, but let's also spend time focusing on that which truly fills our hearts and cares for our souls.

It is my prayer that the pause found on these pages would provide you a moment of peace. A break in the hustle and bustle. A chance to drink deep and savor this fleeting and favored season.

On each of the twenty-five days in this book, you'll find a brief Scripture, a short devotion, a question to ponder, and an "extra shot" – like espresso for your soul! Among the extra shots are inspiring quotes, fun autumn ideas, and nine of my best recipes for you to try (several of them include pumpkin, of course). There's also one bonus devotion to help you welcome Advent.

Here's to experiencing soul-deep, heart-filling moments this season. Here's to spending intentional time with our family and friends during the season of gratitude. Here's to pumpkin-flavored everything!

To autumn,

Anna

PUMPKIN SPICE

For I am convinced that neither death nor life, neither angels nor demons, neither the present nor the future, nor any powers, neither height nor depth, nor anything else in all creation, will be able to separate us from the love of God that is in Christ Jesus our Lord.
ROMANS 8:38

It's no secret. I love all things pumpkin spice. Lattes. Lotion. Cookies. Candles. Pancakes. Bread. Slap a *pumpkin spice* flavor label on it and it'll probably end up in my cart. My friends know about this love affair of mine, and they'll send me little gifts, cards, even t-shirts that talk about pumpkin spice love. I'm amassing quite the collection, and I'm loud about and proud of it all.

Several years ago, I went on a regular grocery trip to Trader Joe's. Little did I know, this trip would impact my life for EVER. (Dramatic capitalization intentional.) Upon walking into the very first aisle of the store, I began noticing different pumpkin items. Turning the corner, I saw even more. Some were displayed prominently on separate end caps, while others were on the regular shelves mixed among the non-seasonal items. I was thrilled and added items to my cart left and right. Fast-forward many years, and this autumn grocery trip has become a tradition. I pick up a pumpkin spice latte on the way to the store, my kids do a little cheer, and I use the hashtag #annasannualpumpkinrun on Instagram.

Oh yes, I do.

One year, after posting a photo on Instagram of the haul from my annual trek, I received a message from a news station. They were hoping I would give them permission to share my photo during their afternoon show's local interest segment. It had been a heavy news day, the reporter explained, and she thought my fun post would lighten the days of the viewers.

Of course, I said yes! People need to know about the existence of pumpkin cinnamon rolls, pumpkin biscotti, pumpkin pasta, pumpkin crackers, pumpkin butter, pumpkin cereal, pumpkin cookies, and pumpkin dog treats – yes, even my dog's in on it. *Share away*, I told the reporter. Share far and wide, spread this pumpkin-y love affair in all the land and bring pumpkin-flavored joy to all!

It occurs to me that as Christians, we also know a secret that could lighten and brighten up the days of those around us. That Jesus of ours; His love is so deep and so wide. Nothing can separate us from that love. No matter what. Forever and ever, amen. It's a love deeper than even my love of all things pumpkin (and that's a deep love, y'all.) This love is powerful and tucked right into our hearts, but sometimes we need a little reminder.

Let's be the reminder to those around us. And let's not let ourselves forget either.

Pray

Lord, thank you for the gift of autumn. As we fill our carts with pumpkin-flavored treats, keep our hearts open and ready to be filled with your love. Help us to share the Truth of that love far and wide. Amen.

Ponder

1. How can you live into the big, deep and wide love of Jesus?
2. What ways can you teach your kids (or family or friends) about His huge love?

Extra Shot

Make up a big batch of these lattes and deliver to your school's teachers' lounge, your church office, or a neighbor. They're spicy, pumpkin-loaded, and delicious. Welcome, pumpkin spice season! We've been waiting for you.

SLOW-COOKER PUMPKIN SPICE LATTE

This is my favorite autumn sipper. It tastes more pumpkin-y and less sugary than most coffee shop pumpkin spice lattes. If you're making this for a gathering, it's simple to double or triple the recipe. It's also easy to customize! Depending on your tastes, use more or less of the coffee, maple syrup, and spices. Any way you make it, I hope you'll enjoy!
Serves 2-3.

Ingredients:

1 cup milk
2 cups strongly brewed coffee
3 Tbsp. canned pumpkin
3 Tbsp. pure maple syrup
2 Tbsp. pure vanilla extract
¼ tsp. pumpkin pie spice
Garnish: whipped cream, cinnamon

Instructions:

1. Combine milk and coffee in a small slow-cooker.
2. With a wooden spoon or rubber spatula, gently stir in pumpkin, maple syrup, vanilla extract and spice until well combined.
3. Cover and cook on high setting for 2 hours, or until warmed through. Keep an eye on your

slow-cooker – some heat up more quickly than others, and you don't want the lattes to scorch. Stir occasionally.

4. When warm, stir and ladle into mugs.
5. Top lattes with whipped cream. This is a non-negotiable, vital part of the recipe. It adds sweetness and creaminess to the latte!
6. Sprinkle with cinnamon.

BACK TO SCHOOL

Intelligent people are always ready to learn. Their ears are open for knowledge. PROVERBS 18:15

God stands with us in the aisles of picked-over school supplies. In the middle of the living room, surrounded by labels yet to be stuck on dozens of those school supplies. In the college dorm room, which was empty when we arrived and now as we drive away, is crammed with instant mac & cheese, twin XL comforters, and our whole heart. Waiting at the bus stop for the very first time.

God stands with us, and He stands with our kids.

We've worked, prepared, packed, and prayed for these days. The backpacks are full. The lunches are packed. Alarm clocks are set, and outfits laid out. Bags have been stuffed, books have been bought, and forms (so. many. forms.) have been filled out.

Some of us are elated. Some of us are fearful. Some of us are teary. Most of us are all of the above.

It does my heart good to remember that God goes first, especially into the places where parents cannot. He goes before. He's ready and waiting for our kids. They do not walk through those doors alone.

I find myself questioning what more I can send with my kids into school to give them peace, love, assurance and confidence. If I read that book to them, they'll remember. If I send a note in their lunch, they'll remember. If I go with them to college and move into their dorm with them, they won't be able to forget. But the only One who can accompany our kids and provide everything they need is standing by them already. With our love tucked in their hearts and God by their sides, we have done all that we can do to prepare our kids for going back to school.

We'll hold their hands while walking into that big brick building, while leading them to the homeschool table, and while walking them into their dorm. We hold their hands and He holds them close.

Pray

May I put my trust in You, Lord, knowing You go before my kid(s) as they head to school. Pave their way, Lord, that they may see You in each and every turn. Help them to make friends, to work hard, to have a mind open and ready for learning beyond their reading & writing. Keep my love tucked deep into their hearts. Help them to be brave and kind, Lord... and help their mom be the same. Amen.

Ponder

1. Growing up, what traditions were important to you on your first days of school?
2. How can you make the day special for your kids without stressing yourself out?

Extra Shot

Host a back-to-school brunch – for the moms! On my oldest child's first day of kindergarten, I knew there was a chance that I would be a complete wreck – and that my mom friends might be, too. So, I invited them all over for a back-to-school brunch! I had muffins, fruit, coffee, and mimosas in the kitchen. I set out boxes of tissues for the moms and toys for the younger siblings. We had a great time of both commiserating and celebrating. Open your door to some back-to-school moms on the first day of school! It's a great way to commemorate a day that's special for the kids – and also for the moms.

BEGINNINGS

Because of the Lord's great love we are not consumed, for his compassions never fail. They are new every morning; great is your faithfulness.
LAMENTATIONS 3:22-23 (NIV)

Mornings are frenzied. I often find myself wishing for peace and calm instead of frantic and frazzled. I want to enjoy the beauty outside of my windows: the red streaks in the late sunrise, the frost on the grass, and the pumpkin on the porch. I would prefer to sip my coffee slowly instead of gulping it as we rush out the door.

I want my kids to notice the beauty that waits just outside of our walls, because then they'll be more apt to notice the wonder inside of our home.

But usually, mornings look more like me barking commands to my kids. "Eat! Shoes! Brush teeth! Don't forget your backpack! Go, go, go!" And the beginning of our day, week, month, season is off and running while I'm flailing to catch up.

So today, I'm beginning in prayer. Nothing fancy or difficult. I can whisper hope for patience and peace before my feet hit the floor. I can bark one more command to get their attention, and we can pray calmly before we eat breakfast. I can connect with Him as I wait in the "parade," as my 4-year-old calls it (really, it's the preschool drop-off line). God and I hang out in the car a lot, right in between cracker crumbs and howling toddlers. The cracks are where I'll find God today, and where I'll accept the peace He offers amidst the chaos.

God says His mercies are new each day, and I'm going to take Him up on that. What a beautiful kind of beginning that could be. As you step into autumn – a whole season of beauty, giving thanks, having fun, and celebrating holidays – may your beginnings be blessed.

Pray

Lord, thank you for new beginnings. May I feel your compassion and new mercy today. May I share such compassion and grace with my kids, co-workers, friends, and family. Autumn is a beautiful way to begin. Amen.

Ponder

1. If you were to truly embrace the new mercy and compassion God offers, how would it change your heart and life?
2. What ways can you extend grace to those around you today?

Extra Shot

Life starts all over again when it gets crisp in the fall.

- *F. Scott Fitzgerald*

HAYRIDES

No one can lay any foundation other than the one we already have – Jesus Christ. Anyone who builds on that foundation may use a variety of materials – gold, silver, jewels, wood, hay, or straw. 1 CORINTHIANS 3:11-12

An autumn hayride usually includes bales of hay or straw, providing a soft and practical place to sit on an otherwise flat tractor bed. The bales present a particularly earthy, nutty smell, and they're often warm after spending a day soaking up the heat from the late autumn sunshine. Sitting on a bale of hay or straw as we're trucked through an orchard is on basically everyone's autumn bucket list.

In addition to the pumpkins we pick up when we visit our local pumpkin patch each October, we always bring home a bale of straw to set out in front of our house. The kids love climbing on it, I love decorating it with a few pretty pumpkins, and we can compost it before winter arrives.

Much more important than a hayride or creative autumnal décor, God found a way to use even hay for His glory.

Paul, author of the letter to the Corinthians referenced above, writes that as long as our foundation is Jesus Christ, we can use whatever we have to build upon it. Now, most stories involving hay or straw make them out to be weak and flimsy building materials. The big bad wolf blows down the little pig's house built of straw, and all that.

But God says if our foundation is firmly in place we can use even hay or straw to build upon it. His foundation is strong enough to withstand the messes we make on top of it. It's the foundation that determines the strength of the structure.

When Jesus is the base, He is what makes our feet stand firm. He provides the solid ground. Whatever we use to build on top of that, He's going to make it work. Are there choices available that are good, better, and best? Of course. But what a relief that the ground work has already been laid down.

On an autumn hayride, the bales of floppy straw or hay hold us steady as we sit on them. Imagine how much more durable a foundation of Jesus is. That's what will solidly hold up our lives, no matter what we throw at it.

Pray

For a firm foundation, I thank you. Even when it feels shaky, You hold my life steady. Lead me toward the best materials for building upon what You have laid down. Amen.

Ponder

1. How steady does your foundation feel?
2. How can you dig in deeper to feel Jesus' strength?

Extra Shot

For a sweet autumn treat, combine equal parts candy corn, roasted peanuts and M&Ms in a bowl. Fill up a bag with this trail mix to sweeten any hayride!

BAKING

But the Holy Spirit produces this kind of fruit in our lives: love, joy, peace, patience, kindness, goodness, faithfulness, gentleness, and self-control.
GALATIANS 5:22-23

One autumn a few years ago, I was in a new and lonely place. My husband and I had moved more than ten hours away to live and work at a Bible camp on the prairies of North Dakota. We were excited about our new jobs, adorable house onsite at camp, and our new dog (we adopted her just days after moving in).

But there were aspects of our new life that were difficult at best. It was painfully hard to be so far away from our families, our work schedules made it challenging to meet people and make friends, and parts of our new life weren't what we'd expected. My heart felt trapped in a permanent state of grief, and I had to learn how to best care for my own self – my heart, my soul, and my emotional well-being. I needed to actually invest time and energy into self-care practices. I needed to start at the very beginning and discern what those practices were. I didn't actually know that's what I was doing – all I knew was that I had to figure out what brought me joy, because I wasn't experiencing any.

Eventually, things that helped soothe and care for my soul became clear. Joy started to return. I began to pay attention to what I was doing when I found myself breathing deeply and feeling calmer, and then I did those things more often. I found joy and solace in three activities especially:

- Taking my dog on a lot of long walks. We walked in crunchy leaves and crunchy snow. We walked on dark evenings and bright mornings. We walked in sunshine, and we walked in rain. We did a lot of walking.
- Listening to the same piano playlist all. year. long. on repeat. It calmed my heart and nerves, and gave my brain space from stress.
- Baking. When I measured and mixed, my heart settled. I baked, and I mailed the product of the feelings-baking to my friends. Because nothing says, "I'm caring for myself," quite like sharing baked goods. There was something profoundly soothing about following an ordered recipe, stirring and sifting, and even waiting to experience the end product. I baked dozens of pumpkin loaves that year.

Over a decade later and my life is completely different. I'm a working mom of young children, active in my church and community, and smack dab in the middle of a wonderful and full life. Along with drinking plenty of water, eating good food, getting enough rest (when I can. I do have three kids so a full night of sleep is a rarity!), I turn to the comfort of those activities from that season long ago.

"Self-care" has become a cultural buzz word since those days. Unfortunately, I've observed that while the importance of and need for actual self-care has increased, our self-care tools have decreased in their helpfulness.

Because when we think we're practicing self-care, often we're actually practicing self-indulgence. Real self-care is not selfish. It's not a waste of time. It's not pedicures. It's not scrolling Facebook. It's not shopping online. It's not chocolate.

Real self-care is deeper than all of that. Real self-care contributes to a well-tended soul, which in turn produces fruit. The fruit of the spirit, if you will.

Self-care, when combined with God's great love, is that which leads us to Peace. Kindness. Gentleness. General goodness. Patience. Joy. Love. And all of these traits lead us to Self-control. Eventually, self-care may equal self-control.

May you begin to notice that which leads your heart to peace. May you lean into the tasks and activities that provide you pure joy. And in the same way pumpkin bread rises when baked, may these fruits bubble up in your heart, ready to be poured out in your home and life.

Pray

Lord, lead me to that which calms my soul and refreshes my heart. Help me discern what brings me peace and joy, and to lean in to those things when they become clear. Thank you for the way you care for me, and the ways you're teaching me to care for myself. Amen.

Ponder

1. What if, instead of a latte break or mindless scrolling, we took time to actually care for ourselves? What would that look like for you?
2. What stumbling blocks do you run into with self-care?

Extra Shot

Schedule an autumn baking session into your calendar. Whether it's by yourself, with your kids, your mom, or a friend, write it on a date in your planner. Choose a recipe, either an old favorite or one that's new and interesting – try mine for the best ever pumpkin bread! Gather the ingredients and give into the order and rhythm of a recipe. Do your best to not be rushed, but to take your time and enjoy the process. Share the delicious final product with your kitchen helpers or a neighbor.

BEST EVER PUMPKIN BREAD

I was gifted this recipe at my bridal shower over thirteen years ago. All these autumns later, and the recipe has never let me down! It's flavorful, well spiced, super moist, and freezes nicely.
Makes two large loaves.

Ingredients:

3 $^{1}/_{3}$ cups all-purpose flour
2 tsp. baking soda
1 $^{1}/_{2}$ tsp. salt
1 tsp. cinnamon
1 tsp. nutmeg
3 cups sugar
1 cup vegetable oil
4 eggs
15 oz. can pumpkin
$^{2}/_{3}$ cup water

Instructions:

1. Preheat oven to 350°. Lightly grease two 5 x 9" loaf pans.
2. Mix the flour, baking soda, salt, cinnamon and nutmeg together; set aside.
3. In a large mixing bowl, place the sugar and vegetable oil; using an electric mixer, beat on high speed until light and well blended.
4. Add eggs to the mixing bowl, beating after each addition until well blended.

5. Add pumpkin and water; beat until completely blended.
6. Add flour mixture in one cup at a time, scraping sides of bowl and beating on low speed after each addition only until blended.
7. Pour batter into prepared loaf pans; spread evenly.
8. Bake 65-75 minutes or until wooden toothpick inserted in center comes out clean.
9. Remove from oven; place on wire racks. Cool for 10 minutes. Remove from pans and let loaves stand on wire racks until completely cool.

AUTUMN REFLECTIONS

ORCHARD

Then God said, "Look! I have given you every seed-bearing plant throughout the earth and all the fruit trees for your food. And I have given every green plant as food for all the wild animals, the birds in the sky, and the small animals that scurry along the ground—everything that has life." And that is what happened. GENESIS 1:29-30

Every autumn of my childhood, my family would drive to an orchard far out in the country. It felt like a magical place. We'd sit on hay bales placed on a flatbed trailer and pulled by a tractor through the rows of Honeycrisp, Gala, Macintosh and Cortland apples, each variety noted with a colorful ribbon tied to the trees. We'd hop off the trailer when we were good and deep in the orchard, then run the rows, climbing into the trees to get apples off branches above our heads. They had a fantastic bakery featuring these amazing caramel apple puff pastries and cider donuts. They pressed cider there in the big barn, and if we were well-behaved our mom would let us walk up an old wooden stairway leading to an observation deck above the press.

We'd watch the apples travel down their runway, go into a washer, bounce along into a platform that seemed to jiggle the dirt right off, go through a peeler, and end in an enormous vat that somehow magically transformed the apples into the delicious cider we took home in gallon jugs.

It was one of my favorite days of the whole year, and it had little to do with the apples. (Now the donuts are another story. I would drive hours for those donuts.) The food and apple picking were a perk of the whole orchard experience – the real joy was found in enjoying creation together with my family.

The Lord has given us everything that has life – including apple orchards, animals, and each other. With one breath God created all that moves and breathes and sings, dances and argues and speaks, swims and jumps and runs.

That includes you and me.

On the days when we feel tiny, insignificant, small and as though we don't really matter very much, we need to remember that each and every breath we take was given by God.

This breath was also gifted to your spouse and your kids. To that guy who cut you off in traffic this morning. To the co-worker who never holds the elevator. It was given to your pastor. Your neighbor. Your college friend who riles people up daily on Facebook. God gave life to each and every person who crosses our paths and to each changing leaf, ray of sunshine, raindrop, and tree branch.

Ours is a God of creativity and fun. I see it in our golden retriever, in our young children, and in every autumn visit to the orchard. Where do you see the creative work of God?

P.S. – In case you're curious, we do still visit that orchard. One year, we showed up for our annual apple orchard day – and it was closed, for good. We were devastated. The next year we received an email telling us that a family had purchased the orchard, and they would be reopening in the fall!

We drove up on opening day and I inhaled a cider donut the minute they handed it to me over the bakery case. All was right with the world again.

Pray

Creative God, thank you for making everything that has life. Thank you for including me and my family among those wonders. Help us glorify and praise You with the very breath You've given us. Amen.

Ponder

1. How does knowing that God breathed life into each of us affect the way you look at yourself? Your spouse? Your kids?
2. Where in nature do you most see and appreciate the joy of the Lord?

Extra Shot

If you don't already have a tradition of going to an apple orchard, start now! Pack a bag with water bottles, wet wipes (apple picking can get sticky), and a fully-charged phone for picture taking. Take a drive, enjoy picking the apples, indulge in cider donuts at the bakery and apples straight from the trees, and have fun!

CRISP

Sing the praises of the Lord, you his faithful people; praise his holy name. For his anger lasts only a moment, but his favor lasts a lifetime; weeping may stay for the night, but rejoicing comes in the morning.
PSALM 30:4-5 (NIV)

My birthday is in the beginning of October, and the joy that this brings me is a little over-the-top. To have a birthday in this season so saturated with beauty and promise feels like the first gift I ever received.

Also, I detest being too warm. Where I live, October weather is generally crisp and cool – right up my alley.

After waking up in the morning, the anticipation of a free pumpkin spice latte from my favorite coffee shop fuels me right out of bed. I've passed along my adoration of holidays and celebrations to my children, so they're almost as excited as Christmas morning when they join me in the kitchen. I open their cards and gifts, then jump into the rush of our regular morning routine.

After school drop-offs, I swing by that coffee shop. I go to work. I make sure to take a walk at some point during the day because to me, outdoors is the best place for my heart to connect with His. On a perfect day, the sky is a brilliant blue and the air holds a hint of a chill in its undercurrent. Of course, I prefer the chill, but year to year the weather varies, and I've worn both tank tops and sweaters on my birthday. We usually have my favorite meal for dinner – fondue! – and family joins us as they're able. When I finally climb into bed at the end of that October day, my heart is full to overflowing with love, filled to the brim with joy.

Did the kids fight or disobey or ask a million questions or interrupt or complain during that day? Um, yes. Did my husband and I probably have a little spat at some point? Most likely. Did we leave the laundry in the washing machine too long and have to re-run it... twice? You betcha. Did I have to run out for diapers and milk and apples? Uh-huh. Were my floors covered in dog hair? For sure.

Was it totally full of joy anyway? Oh yeah!

Joy isn't limited to perfection. If that were the case, we'd all be miserable. Instead, joy can be found in limitless quantities and places. Rejoicing can come every morning – as long as we're open to finding it. I think God wants joy to be as accessible and available as possible. It's why small and seemingly normal things can make our hearts so happy.

It doesn't have to be your birthday to have a day full of joy found in simple, everyday glories. It's autumn! The air is crisp and cool, full of promise, new beginnings, and fresh starts.

On a crisp autumn morning, when joy is ripe for the finding, grab ahold. Look for it around every corner and smile. Seek it in the familiar and the unexpected. And thank the One who created joy, planting it in our hearts and lives.

Pray

Thank you for joy! In the big and in the small, in the normal and the extraordinary and all the spaces in between. Thank you for bringing joy each morning, arriving with the dew. Whether the day is crisp and bright, rainy and grey, or somewhere in the middle... help me seek joy. Amen.

Ponder

1. What everyday glory is bringing you joy today?
2. Do you consider "joy" and "happiness" to be the same thing? Why or why not? If not, what makes them different?

Extra Shot

Crispy air and azure skies,
High above, a white cloud flies,
Bright as newly fallen snow,
Oh, the joy to those who know October!

- *Joseph Pullman Porter*

APPLES

I will make a pathway through the wilderness.
I will create rivers in the dry wasteland. ISAIAH 43:19

Once upon a time, in a not-so-distant past, my family listed our house for sale twice in two years. We moved three times over those two years – first in with my mom, then briefly back to our "sale pending" house, and finally into our new home. During that second year, specifically that autumn, you could say we had a lot going on:

- From August on, our belongings were packed into a storage unit, and our family was packed into my mom's townhome.
- In September I self-published my first book, packing up and mailing out each order from my mom's living room.
- In October we made six offers on six houses, each one turned down.
- In November, my youngest child turned one, and we moved into our new home (the seventh offer we made) just before Thanksgiving.
- My little sister got married on New Year's Eve. I had the pleasure of planning and hosting her bridal shower (in October) and bachelorette brunch (in November).
- Within the last ten days of December, we celebrated my son's fifth birthday, Christmas, and my sister's wedding (in which my family was the ring bearer, flower girls, matron of honor, and groomsman).

So many events were on the calendar that season, and each one fun and important! Recently I was reflecting on that chaotic autumn, and I remembered one morning when I made apple cinnamon oatmeal.

We'd been packing up to move out of our home the next week, so many of the items we use daily were stored away in boxes. I hadn't been doing a ton of cooking because of the inconvenience, but this day while we were in our still-half-ours home, I pulled out my trusty old slow-cooker.

I chopped, measured, poured, and stirred. I rocked out to the music playing from my phone, sitting on a messy kitchen counter. I ran out of non-stick cooking spray and found that the cupboard holding the apple corer was full of crumbs from the toaster. I ruffled heads that ran by and I stooped to hand over a refilled sippy cup. As I prepared the simplest of meals in my very-real-life, never-been-pinned kitchen, I felt peace replace stress in my heart, my shoulders, and my brain.

Frayed nerves soothed, I was calmer. I was able to roll with the little things that sometimes derail my day. I breathed more deeply. I was kinder to my kids and husband. I was motivated at work. I went to bed early, and I was satisfied with how the day had gone.

That day in my half-packed, running-out-of-groceries, crumb-covered kitchen, God gave me a river. A cool, refreshing oasis in a parched land of daily tasks that had dried out my soul. He used twenty minutes of simple meal preparation to create a pool in the bare branches of my heart.

All that, just by taking time to peel and dice a few apples.

God doesn't need much to make much. Ours is a God who makes much of our small offerings. Even when we no longer feel the river of peace or a pathway of clarity, it doesn't mean God has stepped away. The stream doesn't run dry. The path doesn't become overgrown. The branches aren't bare forever. God's love leaves a lingering calm that can reign in our hearts when we feel anything but peaceful.

Pray

Lord, bring your peace. Bring your calm to my heart and day. In a barren landscape, forge a river. Make a new pathway, and make much from my small offerings. Thank you for a new day in which to seek peace and joy. Amen.

Ponder

1. Where can you make space for Him to meet you today – while doing dishes, running errands, or having lunch in your cubicle?
2. Where do you find peace amidst the chaos of your everyday life?

Extra Shot

My slow-cooker is my best friend – and not just at dinnertime. This is my favorite autumn breakfast recipe. Enjoy!

SLOW-COOKER APPLE CINNAMON OATS

This recipe makes a huge batch, so after it's cooked, I put it into a 9 x 13" glass pan, cover it, and keep it in the fridge. In the mornings I scoop out the amount we need and microwave it. A simple, healthy and hearty breakfast for the whole family!

Serves 5, with leftovers.

Ingredients:

1 ½ cups water
1 ½ cups milk
3 cups steel cut oats
2 medium apples, peeled and chopped
¼ tsp. sea salt
1 tsp. cinnamon
2 Tbsp. pure maple syrup
2 Tbsp. ground flax seed

Instructions:

1. Coat inside of slow cooker liberally with non-stick cooking spray.
2. Add all ingredients in their listed order; mix well.
3. Cook for 5-6 hours on low, or 2-3 hours on high. Watch closely while cooking – this stuff burns easily.

FOOTBALL

And the very hairs on your head are all numbered. So don't be afraid; you are more valuable to God than a whole flock of sparrows. MATTHEW 10:30-31

I'm not a big sports person, but I love traditions. I love coming together with a crowd of strangers to cheer for a common goal. I love celebrations of any kind, big or small. I love good food, tailgating, and grilling. I also love a good theme for a party or gathering. With a husband who loves sports and kids who seem to be following in his footsteps, watching and playing sports seems to be becoming a thing in our family.

And football is no exception.

Most autumn Sunday afternoons will find us simmering a pot of chili, donning our home team's colors and cheering with the game on the TV. My kids are old enough to attend a high school football game once in a while, and the pure joy on their faces when they see that packed stadium is worth the price of admission.

It's one way they experience being a part of something much bigger than they are. The music. The green turf. The marching band. The larger-than-life football players in their matching jerseys. Even the scoreboard is giant and fun to watch.

It's fun to be a part of something bigger than yourself, whether you're a cheerleader, a player on the team, in the marching band, or rooting up in the stands. Each of those places needs every single member to boldly, proudly, and loudly do their part. If one horn is missing from the band, their formations and harmonies may fall apart. If one cheerleader is missing from the pyramid, it will fall. If a player is missing from the team, the play can't be completed as practiced. And the stands would be empty if every person thought, "I don't need to go to the game tonight. No one will notice if I'm there anyway."

Your presence matters – probably much more than you know. Without you, things fall apart. It's like doing a puzzle. If one piece is missing, that hole becomes the focal point instead of the bigger picture.

God notices each and every little thing that you may think goes unseen. Every diaper changed. Every text sent. Every meal cooked. Every job completed at work. Every hug and kiss shared. Every sacrifice made.

God sees. God notices. God knows. The Lord knows the number of hairs on your head – He numbered each of them – and you matter deeply to Him. You're not just a face in the stands. You're God's precious daughter.

Pray

Lord, it's so easy to feel overlooked and unseen. Thank you for knowing, seeing, loving me. Amen.

Ponder

1. When have you been a small part of something bigger?
2. How did that make you feel?

Extra Shot

Tailgating at the big game or hosting an autumn get-together? Have a baked potato bar! Scrub and pierce russet potatoes, and pile them in a roaster set to 400°. Bake for an hour or until tender when pierced with a fork. Set out bowls of toppings such as sour cream, bacon bits, chopped chives, diced ham, butter, and broccoli florets. Simple and delicious – even picky eaters will find something they enjoy!

BONFIRES

Let us think of ways to motivate one another to acts of love and good works. And let us not neglect our meeting together... but encourage one another. HEBREWS 10:24-25

I have fond, friend-filled memories of bonfires. Working at a Bible camp as a counselor, we had campfires every single evening of the whole summer. Growing up, we had a portable firepit that welcomed friends often. And last summer, we ripped a funky, gunky koi pond out of our backyard and installed a firepit in its place. I love sitting out there with my husband at the end of the day, and our kids and friends love it too.

One year for my birthday, I gathered a few friends and we met at a local ski hill for an autumn colors sky-ride. We hiked up the hill, then rode the ski lift back down and gazed at the beautiful glory of the trees – the leaves all deep maroon, orange, buttery yellow and scarlet. Up at the top of the hill there was chili for sale, mugs of cider for sipping, and a blazing bonfire next to blanket-covered hay bales and benches. We sat beside that bonfire and talked until they shut the place down for the evening!

Sitting beside a crackling bonfire, wearing a favorite flannel shirt and a winter hat, sipping hot cocoa, and staying toasty while catching up with friends? There's something sacred about that.

When we gaze into the glowing embers of a roaring fire, we're mesmerized. While our eyes feast on the flames, our lips are free to engage in good conversation. The words flow easily, the laughter comes naturally, and the time passes too quickly. Autumn bonfires are a symbol of the coziness and beauty of the season – and they offer the perfect chance to get together with friends.

In a season that's often filled to the brim with school activities and family gatherings, it's so important to make space to gather with friends. Don't neglect meeting together (as the verses above say) even though it's really easy to do so. Our schedules don't line up, the kids have a dozen activities, our calendar is full... press through the inconvenience. It's worth it. Instead of giving up, encourage one another. Be the one to reach out, to organize a get-together, to send the initial text.

Light the fire of friendship and let it blaze.

Pray

Lord, thank you for my friends! They're a gift. A pure present from You to me. Help me be intentional in spending time with them this season; and in the case of neglected friendships, may I both generously extend and receive the gift of grace. Amen.

Ponder

1. What memories do you have attached to autumn bonfires?
2. Some people host a "Friendsgiving" gathering in November – it's a Thanksgiving dinner with a group of friends. What's one way you can make space for friends this season?

Extra Shot

Set a chair next to your back door and stack a pile of warm flannel or knit blankets on it. Not only do the blankets automatically become autumnal décor, they're also practical – grab one on your way to the backyard, and hand them out to friends seated by the bonfire!

AUTUMN REFLECTIONS

PUMPKIN PATCH

"Remain in me, and I will remain in you. For a branch cannot produce fruit if it is severed from the vine, and you cannot be fruitful unless you remain in me. Yes, I am the vine; you are the branches. Those who remain in me, and I in them, will produce much fruit. For apart from me you can do nothing." JOHN 15:4-5

Every autumn, my family visits a local pumpkin patch. Our kids run through the rows of vines snaking the ground and I holler at them to watch where they're going. They take about half an hour to find and choose their perfect pumpkins: round, full, bright orange, no rotten spots, solid stems. We roll the chosen ones onto a cart, pay for them at the counter and bring them home, where we proudly place them on our front steps until it's time for carving. We roast the seeds and snack on them while I make pumpkin bread, and we snap photos of our creations. Our annual pumpkin evenings are so much fun!

When we find something beautiful growing from a thick, rope-like vine, we celebrate it.

Pumpkins are interesting plants. Their vines are prolific growers and will take over the whole yard or patch if they aren't properly pruned. Pumpkins are also rather persnickety in their requirements for growth. They demand a lot of water, good soil and compost, and have a growth period of 75 to

100 frost-free days.[1] Pumpkins thrive because they cling to their vine – their giver of life. They stick tight to it, relying on it for sustenance and nutrients.

A bit of a fuss to raise, but worth it in the end. Because just as you start thinking the whole process was all for naught, you push a great big leaf aside... and there it is. A pumpkin. Something wonderful growing from a vine that is both tender and fierce, protective and wild, fruitful and strong.

People are so much like pumpkins:

- If we cling to the vine, we will grow.
- Sever our connection to the Giver of life and we wither.
- Something wonderful growing from a vine that is tender yet fierce.

Can you even handle the incredible parallels between people and pumpkins?

They're no accident. These ancient verses from John are full of analogies to our own lives. Jesus telling us that He is the vine, and we are the branches – we stem from Him. That we cannot produce fruit on our own – we need to be attached to the One who created fruit in the first place. That He will love us ultimately, remaining in us no matter what. That apart from Him, we really can't do much of anything.

As we visit the pumpkin patch this autumn, hunting for that perfectly orange pumpkin, let God's love slip into your mind. As you choose just

---

[1] *The Old Farmer's Almanac*, https://www.almanac.com/plant/pumpkins

the right pumpkin for your front porch, be reminded that you too have been specially chosen. As the pumpkin brings joy to you and yours, remember that its beauty required a long time to develop. As you showcase your pumpkin for a few autumn weeks until it droops, recall that we too will wither and fade if separated from our Vine.

All of creation breathes theology – even the pumpkin patch.

Pray

May I cling to You, Lord, even when it's hard and You seem far away. Thank You for these words in John – help me to keep them in mind as we visit the pumpkin patch this year. Help me cling to You like a pumpkin to its vine. Amen.

Ponder

1. What "vines" are you clinging to?
2. What makes clinging to God's love easy or difficult for you?

Extra Shot

Sprinkle the inside of a carved pumpkin with pumpkin pie spice. When you place the lit candle inside, your jack-o-lantern will smell delicious!

PUMPKIN CHEESECAKE

I bring this cheesecake to Thanksgiving dinner every year! It's my husband's favorite pumpkin dessert.
Serves 10.

Ingredients:

2 – 8 oz. packages cream cheese, softened
2/3 cup sugar
2 tsp. pumpkin pie spice
2 eggs
15 oz. can pumpkin
1 large prepared graham cracker crust (find this in the baking aisle at your grocery store)
Garnish: whipped cream, cinnamon

Instructions:

1. Preheat oven to 350°.
2. Remove cover from graham cracker crust. Place crust on a jelly roll pan or cookie sheet. This will stabilize the cheesecake and prevent filling from overflowing onto the oven floor.
3. Place softened cream cheese in a medium bowl; beat until fluffy.
4. Add sugar and spice to bowl; beat on medium speed until combined.
5. Add eggs one at a time. Beat on medium speed after each addition.
6. Gently mix in pumpkin. Blend well. Batter may be slightly lumpy.

7. Pour batter into crust.
8. Bake cheesecake at 350° for 40 minutes, until center is set.
9. Cool on wire rack for 10 minutes, then refrigerate at least 3 hours.
10. Serve cold, and top with whipped cream and a dusting of cinnamon.

LEAVES

As long as the earth remains, there will be planting and harvest, cold and heat, summer and winter, day and night. GENESIS 8:22

Here in Minnesota, the sticky-hot, long days of summer stretch deep into September, then finally in October the nighttime and early morning air gives way to a chill.

And that's when the trees know winter is coming. They prepare for it from the inside out.

This knowledge that the trees have feels important, kind of enormous. The trees flourish and reveal their truest selves as their leaves are dying. God has built Truth and theology into trees, and I want to sit at their roots and learn.

How do the leaves know when to drop their guard of green and give into the process of dying to themselves? Why do they trust the timing, each and every year? Do they lean into it, or do they fight back, stubborn in giving into the inevitable blaze of color?

The weather reflects a gradual change. It's cool; the breezes are still; but deep down at their roots, the trees know major change is coming. They know they are to be robing themselves in color, preparing for a brand-new season of beauty – yet some remain green. Are they the ones fighting back, pushing against what they truly are deep inside?

Sounds senseless – to fight for remaining faded and tired instead of bursting gold, red, and orange.

Casting off the wilted end-of-summer green. Embracing what is deep down in the core, the beauty He's placed there to reveal in His time.

Maybe in the middle of our own everyday mess, mixed right into the struggles, He's preparing us for something. Maybe He wants us to choose to take hold, to dig deeper, to look beyond the mess and frustration. To reflect with unquestionable certainty the glory hidden in our hearts because of where He chose to take up residence.

Let's yield to living color, the kind that shines brightest when dying to self has happened first.

Pray

May the change quietly filling the air spark the same in my heart. May I allow it to wash over my life, brightening each nook and cranny, and sweeping the corners clean of staleness. May cool air fill my lungs as I breathe in His grace and breathe out the old. May I learn, embrace, marvel at what the trees know. Amen.

Ponder

1. How can you dig deeper into what God is doing quietly in your heart?
2. In what ways do your life and heart reflect the change in the leaves?

Extra Shot

October gave a party, the leaves by hundreds came.
The chestnuts, oaks & maples, and leaves of every name.

- *George Cooper*

FAMILY

Just as our bodies have many parts and each part has a special function, so it is with Christ's body. We are many parts of one body, and we all belong to each other.
ROMANS 12:4-5

I have two younger siblings. We each have our own mortgages, priorities, careers, families, and friends. We've grown into our talents and gifts, the awkwardness of our tween years long over (thank goodness) and teenage fights long since forgiven. When we get together for birthdays or holidays, we laugh and reminisce while our kids – cousins! – run around the house.

I'm positive there were days that my mother thought these happy moments would never arrive, because when we were younger my siblings and I fought like cats and dogs. We were pretty different, each of us, and at times those differences hindered our relationships. We're all grown up now and issues still crop up from time to time, but we've tried to focus on our similarities, such as:

- We have the same big grin that crinkles up the corners of our eyes.
- The three of us are all slightly terrified of birds (except for cardinals. Our grandma loved cardinals, so they're the one bird we're happy to see.)
- We all feel emotions deeply. Sometimes it confuses us and we laugh when we're really angry or really sad.

We inherited these likenesses, these things that both bring and bind us together. The differences that tore us apart as kids could threaten to do the same to us as adults, so we try to grab hold of the things that connect us while giving thanks that we are not the same. Our relationship as siblings is far from perfect, but it is good. We recognize that we are many parts of one body.

During the holidays, differences don't have to create drama at the dinner table.

We can disagree with one another yet do so with respect. We can decide that we are better together. We can give way to nostalgia, opening a floodgate of warm fuzzies and memories. We can let love cover a multitude of sins.

Not all differences and disputes can be reconciled. Not all relationships can be healed. Family is often complicated at best; this is rarely as showcased in any bigger way than it is at Thanksgiving. But maybe Thanksgiving can be a time to give thanks for the family we have. Thankful for their quirks, choices, and lives just as they are. Thankful for decades or days of shared memories and experiences. Thankful for the gift of each other.

Maybe for you it isn't siblings but instead a cousin, or your mom, or a favorite aunt. Maybe you're estranged from your family with good reasons. Maybe you're just not feeling family these days. That's okay. You're not out a family just because yours may not be close. The thing about being part of the body of Christ is that when you're in, you're in for life... and then forever.

You're never family-less. You are a part of the body, and we all belong to each other.

Pray

For my loud, messy, weird, wonderful family, I give You thanks. You are Maker, Redeemer, Healer, and Provider to all families. Bless those who cannot be together this season, those who would like to be but are unable. And for those who do gather together, bring forth the spirit of Your peace. Amen.

Ponder

1. What are some of your favorite autumn memories involving family?
2. How do you feel like one part of a larger body – either in your extended family or the family of God?

Extra Shot

Have a family game night! Order in pizza or pop a batch of popcorn, choose a board game, and enjoy some together time.

GOLDEN

This is the message we heard from Jesus and now declare to you: God is light, and there is no darkness in him at all.
1 JOHN 1:5

Fields of gold.
Silence is golden.
Worth their weight in gold.
The golden age.

"Golden" has always been used to convey great worth and beauty, and each of the sayings or images listed above do the same. Autumn has a golden hour of its own, and it is particularly glorious. The sun is beginning to dip lower, and it bathes the land in an incredibly beautiful golden light. Unlike summer, the insects aren't pestering in the evening, and the leaves are putting on their best show, and the sunset is wild and fiery.

There's a reason most family photographers want to schedule their sessions during this time of day, toward the late afternoon or early evening. Everyone looks their best during that golden hour, with the sunlight illuminating the turning leaves, the grass, and the families themselves. It's like nature's best filter, softening frames, edges, and sometimes even hearts.

Family photos during the golden hour are priceless, but so are the behind-the-scenes stories. Because what kids are on their best behavior around 5:00 pm? We've had several such photo shoots, and what didn't get captured on camera were the slurps of suckers between frames. The granola bars tossed into outstretched hands in the backseat as we careened to our destination at 4:58 pm. The promise of going out for pizza after pictures. The packet of wet wipes shoved into my pocket for when that sucker dribbles down my toddler's chin and her hair gets stuck in the trail of sticky drool.

Not quite Christmas card moments, but that golden hour is worth it.

The golden hour gives us a glimpse of God's beauty. He's the original Creator, and while we can see that creativity all around us every day, sometimes it seems that God likes to show off. We are the recipients of such glory. Lucky us! The golden hour, when God is light. Pure, radiant, golden light. In Him there is no darkness at all. We can trust His beauty – and we can see it, too. Not a single sunbeam from the light of the golden hour can be hidden. The sunlight bounces off each branch of God's creation, reflecting glory on every surface.

So it is with God's own heart. The golden hour gives us a glimpse into the splendor of God's beauty, character, and very heart. It can be easy to picture God as a fierce judge or heavenly genie, doling out sentences and granting wishes. But really, our God is immeasurably greater than a judge or granter of wishes. Our God is glorious, magnificent, and full of light. Think golden hour, twinkling and shooting stars, flickering fireflies, bolts of lightning, and the glow of a harvest moon – all combined into one brilliant display of grandeur. That's the light in God's heart.

May we embrace it, experience it, linger in it, and give thanks that we can be there for the beauty of the golden hours.

Pray

Lord, help me soak up these precious golden hours. Thank you for this season of autumn, that I may experience Your beauty in such a bold way. May I not miss a minute of this golden life You've gifted me. Amen.

Ponder

1. How can you embrace the golden hour – tonight?
2. How do you picture God? How could the verses from 1 John change that picture?

Extra Shot

Autumn carries more gold in its pocket than all the other seasons.

- *Jim Bishop*

COZY

On the seventh day God had finished his work of creation, so he rested from all his work. And God blessed the seventh day and declared it holy, because it was the day when he rested from all his work of creation.
GENESIS 2:2-3

Cozy can mean different things to different people, but it is fairly synonymous with autumn.

To me, cozy means sipping a warm pumpkin spice latte while sitting in an overstuffed armchair, quilt on my legs, good book in hand. It means a cinnamon spice candle burning in my kitchen. It means darkness descending earlier in the day, beef stew in the slow-cooker, and tucking into home for the night.

It means rest.

How many times have you offered the "too busy" excuse for explaining why you can't rest? Why you can't make time for a girls' night out, or for reading a book, or taking a walk? Ladies. We cannot continue using these as excuses. Because even God rested. God paused.

After working really hard, God took a breather.

It's the first example of self-care we see in Scripture. In the first chapter of Genesis, God has just created everything. Everything! Then the second chapter opens with God finishing up... and resting.

Has anyone ever worked harder than the Creator of the WORLD? The maker of all the things?! No! And God recognized the hard work

He'd done, and all that it took out of Him. No doubt after resting, God was refreshed, refueled, refilled, and ready to get back to work.

And good thing, because the next thing God has to deal with is Adam and Eve. This. is. huge. God rested before caring for His children.

The rest of Genesis chapter 2 describes how God plants the garden of Eden, prepares it for Adam and Eve, teaches them about caring for the Earth, and introduces Adam to the animals. God creates Eve. Then they eat that forbidden fruit and everything falls apart.

Listen. This scripture is a game changer. God worked really hard, and then God rested before caring for His children. We can do the same. Rest is what God practiced, what has been modeled for us. Is rest what we are practicing, what we're modeling for our kids?

Right now, as we stand at the beginning of a full, busy, fun season of celebration, how can we include rest? How can we embrace the inherent coziness of the autumn season? Because either we do it now, or we miss the chance.

Pray

Lord, I am not too busy to rest. Guide me towards cozy places in my home and heart, and help me to care for myself in thoughtful, intentional ways. Thank you for so beautifully modeling this for us all. Amen.

Ponder

1. What spaces in your home can you make cozier?
2. How are you modeling rest for your family?

Extra Shot

This is one of the coziest recipes in my collection. Enjoy!

CRANBERRY-APPLE CRISP

One year while living far away from my family, I discovered this recipe in an old cookbook. During a lonely season this cozy recipe helped my heart heal. We look forward to it every autumn – it's extra delicious with whipped cream and served alongside a mug of hot coffee!
Serves 6.

Ingredients:

3 cups peeled, chopped apples (Granny Smiths work well)
2 cups fresh cranberries
2 Tbsp. flour
1 cup sugar
2 – 1 5/8 oz. packets cinnamon & spice instant oatmeal (or equivalent of instant oatmeal with pumpkin pie spice added to taste)
¾ cup chopped pecans
½ cup flour
½ cup packed brown sugar
½ cup butter, melted

Instructions:

1. Combine first four ingredients.
2. Press mixture gently into 9 x 13" pan.
3. Combine all other ingredients and spoon over fruit mixture.
4. Bake uncovered at 350° for 40 minutes.
5. Let cool slightly before serving.

COOL

Hot tempers start fights; a calm, cool spirit keeps the peace. PROVERBS 15:18 (MSG)

"The sun's not so hot in the sky today," sings James Taylor[2], and for that I give thanks. One reason autumn is my very favorite is that the sun is not as hot as it is during summertime. Autumn weather in Minnesota is perfect. For a few months we no longer have the blistering heat of summer, and we haven't yet welcomed the frigid cold of winter.

When I stumbled across this verse in Proverbs, I found my heart in a Bible verse. I simply do not enjoy being hot. Not when I'm indoors, not when I'm outside, and not in my mind, body or spirit. When I'm hot I sweat, my face turns red, and my stomach rolls. I am not good at being warm. I fare much better in cool weather – and with a cool spirit. And now I have proof that it's biblical!

Okay, maybe not quite. But the verse can be helpful for those of us who struggle with temper. Did you ever notice that the word *temper* is also in the word *temperature*? There is actually a direct correlation with anger and temperature. There's a reason that we flush red when we're irate, that *blood-boiling* is a description of what rage feels like, and that the color red signifies anger.

---

[2] James Taylor. *October Road.* Columbia Records, 2002. Spotify: http://bit.ly/OctoberRoad.

A cool temper is the exact opposite of out-of-control wrath. And peace is the antithesis of fighting. Is it easy to cool off? Not at all. Is it worth it to take a deep breath and choose peace? Nearly every time.

Now, don't write off the righteous, table-turning kind of anger that flares up with injustice and actual wrongdoing. Even Jesus leaned into such anger[3], and when it's appropriate we should too. But in our general day-to-day dealings, it may serve us well to pause, take a deep breath, and pray for the coolness of peace to enter our hearts.

As the weather itself cools, may our tempers reflect the shift in temperature. May we practice cooling down our spirits. May our hearts remain temperate and kind as we dress in our flannels to ward off the chill in the air. And may we bend toward peace every day of this season.

Pray

Lord, help me to cool and calm myself when I feel my temper flaring. Help me to feel the righteous kind of anger at that which is unjust and wrong. Give me the wisdom to discern between the two. Amen.

Ponder

1. Do you prefer the heat of summer or the coolness of autumn? Why?
2. How do you calm yourself when your temper threatens to flare?

---

[3] Matthew 21:12-13.

Extra Shot

For the last few years on Halloween night, I've filled a huge old-fashioned coffeepot with hot chocolate, set it out on the porch alongside disposable travel cups with lids, and placed a sign next to it that reads, "Adults, help yourselves!" As parents bring their kids door-to-door to gather candy, they can treat themselves to a cup of hot cocoa. It warms both hands and hearts on a cool night, and it's a great way to make a few neighborhood friends.

AUTUMN REFLECTIONS

BOOTS

So, chosen by God for this new life of love, dress in the wardrobe God picked out for you: compassion, kindness, humility, quiet strength, discipline. Be even-tempered, content with second place, quick to forgive an offense. Forgive as quickly and completely as the Master forgave you. And regardless of what else you put on, wear love. It's your basic, all-purpose garment. Never be without it.

COLOSSIANS 3:12-14 (MSG)

At the first hint of a chill in the air, I pull on cute leather boots, jeans, and a sweater. Basically my autumn uniform, I suit up in it most days.

I have this one pair of fabulous boots. Leather, ankle-high with a low heel, they look amazing with my favorite jeans. At 8:00 am, I have high hopes for those boots. I keep thinking this will be the day they won't kill my feet and require swapping them out for flats by 11:00am.

And each day, I'm so wrong.

It's disappointing, not being able to wear those boots more than a few hours before my feet call it quits. But while I love a cute pair of shoes, I also love not being in pain, so back into the closet they go at 11:00 am. Sometimes it's hard to choose another pair, even though I know the boots are not the best for me. They're just so cute!

More difficult than pulling on boots is pulling on the one item Colossians says to be sure and wear: love. Colossians says that regardless of what else you put on, we must wear love. It's our basic, all-purpose garment. Never be without it.

When we pull on love, we can wear it loud and proud. When we pull on love, we can fully know that it won't let us down by 11:00 am like those darn boots. When we pull on love, we can trust God's promises. When we pull on love, we'll be clothed in the richest garment possible.

Maybe today, I'll wear the slightly-less-cute-but-much-comfier boots. As I pull them up and head downstairs to greet the chaos of the morning, I'll remember what I've chosen to wear first. When I pull on love, choosing to let it guide my steps more faithfully than my cutest boots, the path I take will lead me straight to all the compassion, kindness, humility, gentleness, and patience I need for the day.

Pray

Lord, help me choose to wear love today – even when it's uncomfortable or difficult. Guide and lead me to your path, covering all that I say and do in love. Remind me throughout the day of the holy clothing I chose to put on first, and that those garments will never rip, tear or wrinkle. And help me keep them on past 11:00 am. Amen.

Ponder

1. What gets in your way of wearing love?
2. How can you continue to seek compassion, kindness, humility, and quiet strength on the days they don't easily pull on?

Extra Shot

Tall boots folding over in the closet? Take a pool noodle leftover from summer swims and cut it in half. Stick half of the noodle in each boot, and your boots will stand straight and tall in your closet!

TRICK OR TREAT

You made all the delicate, inner parts of my body and knit me together in my mother's womb. Thank you for making me so wonderfully complex! Your workmanship is marvelous—how well I know it. You watched me as I was being formed in utter seclusion, as I was woven together in the dark of the womb. You saw me before I was born. Every day of my life was recorded in your book. Every moment was laid out before a single day had passed. How precious are your thoughts about me, O God. They cannot be numbered! I can't even count them; they outnumber the grains of sand. PSALM 139:13-18

In our home – both growing up and currently – Halloween is a fun day of silly costumes and candy. My mom always made our costumes, and I remember dressing up in a poodle skirt as a 50's girl one year, and wearing a poufy tulle princess skirt another. My kids have gone trick-or-treating as a knight, a unicorn-riding princess, a "fierce" baby dragon, Curious George, the man in the yellow hat, Olaf, Elsa, and one year they dressed as the newspaper-peddling kids in *Newsies*.

We light up our pumpkins and hand out candy before taking to the streets of our neighborhood, where we walk with friends and family until our fingers are too cold to continue. We head home and gather in front of our fireplace, where my kids dump out their heavy treat bags and take stock of all their loot while *It's the Great Pumpkin, Charlie Brown* plays in the background.

I have two rules for Halloween: we don't trick or purposefully frighten each other or anyone else, and we don't hide who we are behind a mask. These are rules for our regular days as well.

The temptation to wear a mask (metaphorically, of course) is all too real and present in our lives. We hide behind all kinds of masks: Instagram filters, Facebook perfection, the "I'm too busy" excuse, even work. All of these things can be worn as masks, hiding who we are.

The thing is, who we really are has no need to be hidden. God has already told us who we are. Very clearly, God says we are:

- Good.
- Very good.
- Beloved.
- A temple for His heart.
- Remembered.
- Rejoiced over.
- More than a conqueror.
- Holy.
- Redeemed.
- Beautiful.
- Forgiven.

No tricks. Just truth.

We belong to the One who knit us together, who saw us before we were born, who knows each and every one of our complexities and days and hairs. We belong to the One who thinks of us more than there are grains of sand. Hear that again: the number of times God thinks about you outnumbers the grains of sand.

That's who we are. We are thought of. We are loved. And we never have to hide behind a mask.

Pray

If this is who You say I am, Lord, I will work to believe it. Thank you for thinking of me so often; it's overwhelming in the best way. Amen.

Ponder

1. Is it easy or difficult for you to take off your mask and embrace who God says you are? Why?
2. How can you help your friends and family believe they can remove their masks and believe in who God says they are?

Extra Shot

I make this meal every year on Halloween night. It's easy to put together while kids are putting on their costumes, and it includes some extra veggies for filling up bellies before trick-or-treating!

TRICK OR TREAT SLOPPY JOES

I make these sandwiches on Halloween night to get something besides candy into my kids. These taste like a real treat but sneaking in healthier lean ground turkey and bell peppers makes them a little tricky! Served on whole wheat buns with a side of mixed veggies, this is one trick your family won't mind.

Serves 5.

Ingredients:

1 tsp. olive oil
1 medium onion, chopped
1 medium red bell pepper, chopped
2 cloves garlic, minced
1 lb. ground lean turkey
½ tsp. sea salt
¼ tsp. ground black pepper
1 cup tomato sauce
1 Tbsp. Worcestershire sauce
1 Tbsp. pure maple syrup

Instructions:

1. Heat oil in a large skillet over medium heat.
2. Add onion and bell pepper; cook until onion is translucent (about 4-5 minutes), stirring frequently.
3. Add garlic; cook for one minute, stirring frequently. Transfer onion mixture to medium bowl; set aside.

4. Add turkey to same skillet; cook over medium heat for 8-10 minutes until no longer pink, stirring to break up turkey.
5. Season turkey with salt and pepper.
6. Add onion mixture, tomato sauce, Worcestershire sauce, and maple syrup to skillet. Mix well.
7. Reduce heat to medium-low and simmer for 15-20 minutes until sauce has thickened.
8. Stir and serve!

BLANKETS

Love each other with genuine affection, and take delight in honoring each other. ROMANS 12:10

In 2015 we had a newborn, a two-year-old and a four-year-old. My husband and I hadn't eaten a meal at its proper temperature all year, or slept uninterrupted, or done enough laundry, or kept up with friends. We listed our house for sale right before our youngest was born, then we re-listed it when she was seven months old, then moved in with my mom over the summer and didn't move out for six months. Our youngest daughter's entire first year was change.

In October of that year, we scheduled a family photo session with our trusted family photographer. Sarah has documented our kids on their first few days of life, then at six months, and again at one year. She's also taken our family photos in between. She always manages to capture *us* – the real us, just as we are, but also somehow completely beautiful.

That fall, we met Sarah in an open field during the "golden hour." The light from the setting sun played off greens and yellows in the grasses, bounced off the red sumac, and lit up the orange leaves. She placed our family on an old quilted blanket. Even our family dog laid on it. The kids were fidgety but adorable, and we hoped she got a few gems from our time together on that blanket.

A few weeks later she sent us the gorgeous final images. She also included a note that read, "I hope these serve as a reminder that all that really truly matters fits on a blanket."

This simple statement brought me straight to tears with its poignant truth. Especially as we'd been living out of suitcases, everything else we owned crammed into a storage unit and we ourselves stuffed into one room, Sarah's words took on new meaning.

When all is in upheaval, when everything is upended, without rhythm, and life is twisty, look to your blanket.

This week, amidst the crazy to-do list and very beginning of the overloaded and busy holiday season, how can you wholeheartedly and fully pay attention to the people on your blanket?

Pray

Thank you, Lord, for those You've placed on my blanket. Bless them today. Give us time together (whether in person, via texting or pictures on Instagram) to love and appreciate one another.

Ponder

1. Who sits with you on your blanket?
2. How do you connect with the people who are in your corner? How can you connect with them this season?

Extra Shot

The beauty that shimmers in the yellow afternoons of October, who could ever clutch it?

- *Ralph Waldo Emerson*

HARVEST

If you listen obediently to the commandments that I am commanding you today, love God, your God, and serve him with everything you have within you, he'll take charge of sending the rain at the right time, both autumn and spring rains, so that you'll be able to harvest your grain, your grapes, your olives. He'll make sure there's plenty of grass for your animals. You'll have plenty to eat.
DEUTERONOMY 11:13-15 (MSG)

Throughout the brief period of time that my husband and I lived on the plains of North Dakota, we visited many churches as ambassadors of the Bible camp we worked for. We met so many wonderful people, drank a lot of great coffee in church fellowship halls, and saw God's glory across the wide expanse of North Dakota sky.

During one particular church visit that autumn, we were sitting in a wooden pew toward the front of the sanctuary. It had been a lovely service that included several favorite hymns, a robust "greeting of your neighbor," and was now concluding with the prayers. As the pastor led us, he prayed a few sentences about one particular topic (church liturgy calls this a *prayer petition*) and the congregation responded to each with, "Lord, in your mercy, hear our prayer." None of this liturgy was new to me. However, my ears perked up when he began a petition focused on the harvest.

He prayed for the right amount of rain – that neither flooding nor drought would damage the local fields. He prayed for daylight to last longer so the farmers could accomplish as much work as possible during the swift daytime hours. He prayed for a healthy harvest, a fruitful return on years of hard work and backbreaking labor.

Praying for the harvest was new to me, as I'd been born and raised in the suburbs. As I peeked around at those praying around me, it gripped my heart to see their faces upturned and clenched, their hands tightly folded, and their heads nodding in agreement with the petition.

The whole prayer experience only lasted about three minutes and occurred more than ten years ago now, yet I've never forgotten it. Each year when harvest season arrives, I pray for farmers – for the sun to shine, the rain to fall appropriately, the labor of their hands to be prosperous, and for a rich reward for all their work.

We may not all be farmers, but we can certainly pray for an abundant, beautiful harvest in our own lives. Isn't that what we hope for – in our mothering, family, marriages and friendships? Proof of the hard work we've done, the care and attention we've lavished, and the focus and determination it took along the way?

Every farmer knows the result isn't entirely up to them. They can love and care for their fields and still, the crops can be wiped out by a flood, drought, insect infestation or other act of nature. Every mother knows this too – that she can pour her whole heart into raising her kids and they still may not turn out the way she had hoped. Nature takes its course and we can simply nurture the results.

Whatever the harvest may yield, God promises to care for us and for those we love. To provide all that we truly need. And to send the rain at the right time.

Pray

Lord, help me trust the harvest. You hold it in Your hands, and they are more than capable of producing a fruitful crop. Bless the farmers in this season of stress and labor. Amen.

Ponder

1. Do you trust God to provide all that you truly need? Why or why not?
2. What are you harvesting in your life, in your marriage, in your work, in your children?

Extra Shot

Carve out the stem section of a mini-pumpkin (you can use a large drill bit, or a carving knife.). Insert an electric taper candle in the hole, and voila! You have a beautiful and non-flammable harvest time decoration. I like to use several different pumpkins and gourds, placing them in the center of my dining room table and using both taper and tealight electric candles.

AUTUMN ESSENTIAL OIL DIFFUSER BLENDS

A slightly different kind of recipe, these are for your essential oil diffusers. We use essential oils in our home and have found that these combinations smell just like autumn! Adjust quantities to your preference.

Pumpkin Spice:
- 5 drops Cinnamon
- 1 drops Clove
- 1 drop Nutmeg

Pumpkin Pie:
- 2 drops Orange
- 2 drops Cinnamon
- 2 drops Clove
- 2 drops Nutmeg

Thanksgiving Day:
- 2 drops Sandalwood
- 2 drop Siberian or Balsam Fir
- 4 drops Cypress

Spiced Cider:
- 4 drops Orange
- 3 drops Cinnamon
- 3 drops Ginger

Sweater Weather:
- 3 drops Orange
- 3 drops Frankincense
- 2 drops Cinnamon

Halloween Night:
- 2 drops Pine
- 2 drops Frankincense
- 1 drop Lavender
- 1 drop Patchouli

Autumn Morning:
- 2 drops Grapefruit
- 2 drops Orange
- 1 drop Basil

Chai Spice:
- 4 drops Cardamom
- 1 drop Cassia (or cinnamon)
- 1 drop Clove
- 2 drops Ginger

Crisp Fall Air:
- 2 drops White Fir
- 2 drops Orange
- 1 drop Cinnamon

PUMPKIN PIE

For where two or three gather in my name, there am I with them. MATTHEW 18:20 (NIV)

Growing up, my brother, sister, and I spent most Thanksgivings with our dad. The turkey was fine, but we were really there for the pie. He always made a minimum of five pies – apple, French silk, pecan, and two pumpkin pies.

My dad is the pumpkin pie king. Not only has he perfected his recipe, but he makes it frequently. Also, when my dad makes pumpkin pie, he makes more than one. And the extra pie is fully intended to be eaten for breakfast.

Whatever else the day with dad held, my siblings and I knew how the day would begin and most likely end when we walked into his house smelling of pumpkin pie spice and crust, baking away. Bookended by pie, those days.

We connected over pumpkin pie, because my dad and I both love this squash like it's going out of style (which it is not and never will. Amen.) Of all things, it was a pumpkin pie that fostered conversation and laughter.

That pie served as a gateway to love, and anytime love is in the room, so is Jesus. No matter what our gatherings look like, Jesus can show up. In our family rituals and traditions, He is there.

A season heavy with family gatherings and commitments isn't always refreshing and enjoyable. Let's be honest – family is oftentimes complicated at best. Rather than fighting against our family and their quirks, embrace them. Be present if it isn't painful (fully realizing not all families can be together in the same way), and protect your heart if need be. But if it's misunderstandings, miscommunications, disagreeing about politics and parenting styles... love can cover a multitude of spats.

Looking for the common ground helps. Seeking Jesus' face among our family members helps. Eating pie for breakfast helps.

And if it's pumpkin pie, all the better.

Pray

No matter what a day brings, bring me to a common thread with my family. And if we can't find common ground, give me peace. Help me release any guilt I hold from the lack of perfection in my family's dynamics. Help me see Your face among theirs. Amen.

Ponder

1. What common threads run through your family?
2. How do you best connect with your extended family? What ways are you intentional about growing those relationships?

Extra Shot

This is it. Here it is. My Dad's family-famous pumpkin pie recipe, written here in his own words. We hope you enjoy it as much as we do!

DAD'S PUMPKIN PIE

Dad says, "Best enjoyed for breakfast, with coffee. This is based on the recipe from the back of the Festal Golden Pumpkin Pie Filling can – a Minnesota staple at Thanksgiving. It really is the best. Google 'Festal Pumpkin Pie Filling' for the story – it's exciting."

Ingredients:

9" deep dish pie shell
3 eggs, partially beaten
½ cup granulated white sugar
½ cup light brown sugar
¼ tsp. salt
1¼ tsp. pumpkin pie spice
¼ tsp. cinnamon
15 oz. can pumpkin
10 oz. evaporated milk

Instructions:

1. Preheat oven to 350°.
2. Bake crust for 10-15 minutes, until crust is light golden brown. Remove pie crust from oven and set on cooling rack.
3. Turn oven up to 450°.
4. Combine eggs, both sugars, salt, and spices in a large bowl. Beat very well – they tend to stick together in crunchy little clumps.
5. Blend in the beautiful orange pumpkin.
6. Add evaporated milk and beat until your arm tells you, "Enough!" Batter should be a uniform

color throughout, without any dark streaks of spices.

7. Pour mixture into the prebaked pie crust shell. Wipe away any filling that spills onto the crust edge – otherwise it will burn!
8. Bake at 450° for 15 minutes, then reduce oven to 350° and bake for 50-60 minutes. Check doneness by poking a toothpick in the center – the pie is done if the toothpick comes out clean and dry.

Dad's Tips:

- I like to double the recipe and fill several well-greased (with non-stick cooking spray) custard cups. I love the crystalized pumpkin "crust" this creates!
- It is much easier to use a combination pumpkin pie spice than store separate containers of cinnamon, clove, nutmeg, ginger, and allspice.
- If your spices are left over from last year, pitch 'em. Fresh spices truly make a difference in a pumpkin pie.

AUTUMN REFLECTIONS

FEASTS

For the Kingdom of God is not a matter of what we eat or drink, but of living a life of goodness and peace and joy in the Holy Spirit. ROMANS 14:17

My grandma was an excellent cook, and she welcomed me into the sanctuary of her kitchen. She taught me tricks for perfect mashed potatoes, how to make a Sunday roast, and that frozen lasagna is perfectly acceptable for company dinner. She set a beautiful table with her china, and she made a mean gravy from scratch. Holiday feasts at Grandma's included everything, from relish trays to rolls, a main course to several side dishes, and always a mouthwatering dessert.

Grandma never wrote down her recipes. She was very much a "pinch of this, dash of that" kind of cook. After she died, I came across a binder full of recipes she'd assembled from newspaper clippings, recipe cards from friends, and notes she'd jotted down at church potlucks. I even recognized a few dishes that she'd made with me at her side! I loved finding this treasure. Although she'd completely doctored up the actual recipes as she made them, the binder still brought me comfort and continues to do so from its spot on a shelf in my kitchen.

You see, it was never about the feasts she prepared. I mean, her food was amazing. But it was really about being with her. It was about spending time together, standing side by side at the stove. It was about my family gathered around her table, laughing and sharing stories. Going to Grandma's house for dinner was never really about the food; it was about being in the presence of goodness, peace, and joy.

That's what she really left behind for us to inherit. The memories of her goodness, her peace, and her joy are what endure. These are the legacies we will leave our kids, family, and friends.

So write down those special recipes. Share your kitchen space with your kids. Invite family and friends to your table for the feasts of the season. And recognize the intangible gift and goodness that comes from being together, for this is the glory of the Kingdom.

Pray

Lord, thank You for the memory of family feasts. Thank you for those who paved the way with what matters most. In a season of gatherings and meals and feasts, may we remember that it's not really about the food. Amen.

Ponder

1. How can you release yourself from the stress and pressure that often accompany holiday gatherings?
2. What intangible legacy do you hope to leave your family and friends?

Extra Shot

Tips from my grandma's kitchen:

- When making mashed potatoes, cut the potatoes into big chunks before boiling to cut down on cooking time.
- Don't shy away from shortcuts. They allowed Grandma to spend more time with those gathered around her table – frozen lasagnas, pre-chopped veggies, and bakery-fresh rolls were staples in her home. Feel free to use the same.
- Always leave a stick of butter in a covered dish on the counter. That way you're sure to have room temperature butter available when it's called for in a recipe.

TURKEY

Don't worry about tomorrow, for tomorrow will bring its own worries. Today's trouble is enough for today.
MATTHEW 6:34

Let's talk turkey. All food, really. And hospitality. Because autumn, food, and hospitality go together like apple crisp and vanilla ice cream, turkey and stuffing, bread and butter. There's just something about inviting people in for a meal or a treat that gives all the warm fuzzies.

I could tell you to do a day of freezer cooking to help you on those busy practice-chauffeuring, homework-loaded weeknights. I could rave about holiday cookie exchanges with friends. I could share tips for cleaning when company's coming. But the best hosting tip I have actually comes from scripture. The verses apply to much more but are spot on for hospitality as well.

They come from the book of Matthew, chapter 6 [emphasis mine]:

"I tell you not to worry about everyday life—whether you have enough food and drink, or enough clothes to wear. Isn't life more than food, and your body more than clothing? Look at the birds. They don't plant or harvest or store food in barns, for your heavenly Father feeds them. And aren't you far more valuable to him than they are? Can all your worries add a single moment to your life [or to your holidays]?

So don't worry about these things, saying, 'What will we eat? What will we drink? What will we wear? [How will all our tasks get done?]' These things dominate the thoughts of unbelievers, but your heavenly Father already knows all your needs. Seek the Kingdom of God above all else, and live righteously, and He will give you everything you need. So don't worry about tomorrow, for tomorrow will bring its own worries. Today's trouble is enough for today."

This text is the key to peacefully hosting a Thanksgiving (or any other) gathering.

So the bathroom didn't get scrubbed.

So there's still dog hair under the kitchen table.

So the pie burned.

So what. Just open your door and invite your people inside without shame.

Pick up a pie at the bakery. Ignore the dust bunnies. Ditch the extra shopping trip for ingredients and raid your pantry or fridge for leftovers instead. Or order a pizza. Or swing into the drive-through. Commit to the turkey on Thanksgiving and assign all the side dishes to guests.

This scripture passage tells us what our kids' favorite ice queen has been made famous for saying: *Let. it. go.* And do what YOU need to do to enjoy this season in its entirety – from falling leaves to bare branches.

Pray

Lord, help me to focus on the main things and let go of all the rest. Really, all of it. Hospitality is not entertaining, and I ask You to help me be more mindful of that this season. May I model this for my family and friends and release any hesitation I have in flinging open my door.

Ponder

1. What can you release this season in order to more fully enjoy it?
2. What tasks or obligations can you let go of to free up space both in your calendar and your heart?

Extra Shot

For a delicious turkey, baste your bird every 45 minutes with good-quality butter. This will result in golden, crispy skin and juicy meat... simply the best!

DAY-AFTER-THANKSGIVING SOUP

Growing up, my mom made this turkey soup every year after Thanksgiving. She always added frozen egg noodles – they're the secret to making this a hearty, comforting meal. This soup is simple to prepare and perfect for the day after Thanksgiving, as it uses leftover turkey.
Serves 8.

Ingredients:

2 Tbsp. butter
1 large onion, chopped
2 medium carrots, chopped
2 medium celery stalks, chopped
2 cloves garlic, minced
2 quarts turkey or chicken broth
1 – 24 oz. package frozen egg noodles (I prefer Reame's brand)
4 cups cooked turkey, cut into bite-sized pieces
Salt
Ground black pepper

Instructions:

1. In a large soup pot, melt the butter over medium heat.
2. Add the onion, carrots, celery; cook until onion is translucent, about 5 minutes, stirring frequently.
3. Add garlic; cook for one more minute, stirring frequently.

4. Add the broth and bring to a boil.
5. Reduce the heat to low and simmer until vegetables are nearly tender, about 35 minutes.
6. Bring soup back up to a boil. Add frozen egg noodles; stir noodles to separate. Gently boil for another 20 minutes.
7. During the last 5 minutes, stir in the cooked turkey. Season soup with salt and pepper to taste. Serve nice and hot.

STILL

Be still and know that I am God. PSALM 46:10

"You're so busy!" was a phrase I heard often. It occurred to me that I must have been visibly wearing stress, almost as a badge of honor.

When I walked into a room, I'd be huffing and puffing at the circus act that it takes to bring three kids anywhere. Yeah, it usually is a sweaty mess because there are often three bags to carry, three car seats to unbuckle, three jackets to zip kids into, six shoes to Velcro or tie, a double stroller to set up, and one mom juggling it all. But I'm no different than any other mom of tiny children, and most of my friends seemed much calmer when arriving.

I'd hustle us from home to school to drive-thru to activity to home, and then from task to task to task. Our days didn't include anything besides preschool, kindergarten, and church, but they were more than full once we added in meals, snacks, laundry, vacuuming up dog hair, getting people dressed, packing lunches, work, and all the other daily items that cropped up. I realized that if we continued to set a precedent of hustling and hurrying through our days, we wouldn't be set up for success; instead, that kind of schedule would destroy us.

I'd been sacrificing the holiness of everyday moments for the rush of hustled minutes, and I was not okay with that.

I began to see that slow is holy. That everything holy, ancient, and worthwhile is slow:

- Prepping real food
- Cooking real food
- Growing people
- Growing a garden
- Changes of season
- Changes of heart

All holy. All ancient. All worthwhile. All slow. Not a single one can be hurried through.

This is no accident. God has not called us to rush and hurry through our days. He's called us to be still. In so many words, in SO many scripture verses —

- Psalm 23 promises that He will lead us beside still waters, and faithfully restore our souls.
- Psalm 46:10 implores us to be still, and to know that He alone is God.
- Exodus 14:14 declares that if we are still, He will fight for us.
- 1 Samuel 12:16 bids us to stand still so we can see what He's going to do.
- Psalm 37:7 reminds us to be still and wait patiently for Him, even as others seem to be succeeding and moving ahead.

I've been slowing the hurried life I was forcing onto my family. Clearing space on the calendar – making room for friends, family, and grace. Writing fewer to-do's on my task list. Drinking more water and eating good food. Taking walks through the neighborhood as a family, reading more books at bedtime, and soaking in our time together.

At the end of the day, when I close my eyes and let my head hit the pillow, I don't want to look back through a day filled with hurry. I want to scroll the images in my mind, see love lived slowly, and with a soul that is still.

Pray

Lord, as autumn bursts into its full glory and the holiday season starts creeping up, there's no better time to slow my cadence. May I give You the space to do what You can only accomplish in my stillness. May I heed Your call to be still. And may I lean into the holiness of slow. Amen.

Ponder

1. How can you lean into the stillness of this fleeting season?
2. What areas of your life can you intentionally slow down?

Extra Shot

I loved autumn; the season of the year that God seemed to have put there just for the beauty of it.

- *Lee Maynard*

THANKSGIVING

Jesus Christ is the same yesterday, today, and forever.
HEBREWS 13:8

For many of us, Thanksgiving Day holds more traditions than the rest of the year combined. From the Macy's Day Parade to the pumpkin pie, the day is steeped in long-standing, deeply rooted traditions.

In our house, we start with a run to the nearest gas station for three newspapers. Our local paper prints a full-page turkey for kids to color, so three kids = three papers. I grew up coloring that newspaper turkey, and now my kids spend their first hours of Thanksgiving doing the same. While they color, I separate out the ads I want to look at after dinner. We turn the parade on TV, and I start cooking.

Whether we host or visit someone else's home on Thanksgiving, I cook as much as possible that day. I love preparing Thanksgiving foods! The planning (which I usually begin in August) and prepping, shopping and chopping, whisking and basting... I love it all. There are traditions behind the dishes we prepare on Thanksgiving, of course. Mashed potatoes and made-from-scratch gravy are a must. A roasted turkey, both homemade and canned cranberry sauces, and green beans in some form have to grace the table.

While I cook, my family cleans their bedrooms and vacuums the house, getting it ready for the next day (that's when we'll set up our tree and start decorating for Christmas!) We watch whatever football game is on, and after that we switch to the DVD player and put in *A Charlie Brown Thanksgiving*. We may go over the river and through the woods to visit relatives, or they may come to our house; either way, we usually get together with family.

Traditions can keep us close even when our gatherings or hearts are far apart.

We can make the same sweet potatoes we had as kids. We can play football or take a walk after Thanksgiving dinner like we used to do with our siblings or cousins. We can color the newspaper turkey. We can lean on the things that have remained over the years; in fact, it's important that we do.

Author of the *4 Keys for Practicing Faith*, Rev. Dr. David Anderson defines these vital practices as "Rituals and Traditions: Symbolic actions grounded in the Christian tradition throughout the year, providing a beautiful and holistic way of experiencing the grace of God."[4] I love this definition because it validates the value found in incorporating and recognizing traditions in our holidays (and regular days, too!). It also gives weight to the feelings that accompany traditions when they're present, and when those traditions are missing.

I think Jesus has a soft spot for rituals and traditions because He understands how grounding

---

[4] Rev. Dr. David Anderson of Milestone Ministry. *The Four Keys for Practicing Faith*. https://milestonesministry.org/history-of-the-four-keys/

they are to us, His children. He has let us know that He Himself is unchanging, a constant presence on which we can rely. Yesterday, today, and forever – no matter what, He is the same.

He is our greatest tradition.

Pray

I am grateful for the blessings You lavish. For the big ones – family, friends, food, and shelter – and the glory found in the small things as well. Thank You for a day focused on giving thanks. May my life become one of traditions and thankful days. Amen.

Ponder

1. What are some of your favorite Thanksgiving traditions? How did they begin?
2. Why is it so comforting to know that Jesus never changes?

Extra Shot

For a pretty and super-easy Thanksgiving table runner, lay out a long piece of butcher paper along the length of your table. Set crayons or colored pencils next to each place setting, and let guests doodle their own decorations on the paper runner! Or invite each guest to write down what they're thankful for, then after the meal is cleared go around and read what each person wrote.

BACON & BROWN SUGAR GREEN BEANS

I first enjoyed these green beans when my friend Patty made them for a holiday party. We used to be a green bean casserole family, but since have switched over to these at our holiday meals. They are sweet, salty, and totally addictive.

Serves 6-8.

Ingredients:

4 – 12 oz. bags of frozen green beans, thawed
12 slices of bacon, cooked crisp and diced (Pro tip: use a pair of kitchen shears to cut the cooked bacon into bite-size pieces!)
$^{2}/_{3}$ cup brown sugar
$^{1}/_{4}$ cup butter, melted
7 tsp. reduced sodium soy sauce
1 $^{1}/_{2}$ tsp. garlic powder

Instructions:

1. Preheat oven to 350°.
2. Place thawed and drained beans in a 9 x 13" metal or glass pan.
3. Sprinkle the bacon over the top of the beans.
4. In a small bowl, mix together brown sugar, melted butter, soy sauce and garlic powder. Pour mixture over the beans and bacon.
5. Bake for 40 minutes.
6. Toss, and serve warm.

BONUS DEVOTION FOR ADVENT

And because Joseph was a descendant of King David, he had to go to Bethlehem in Judea, David's ancient home. He traveled there from the village of Nazareth in Galilee. He took with him Mary, to whom he was engaged, who was now expecting a child. And while they were there, the time came for her baby to be born. She gave birth to her first child, a son. She wrapped him snugly in strips of cloth and laid him in a manger, because there was no lodging available for them. LUKE 2:4-7

Let's talk about Mary, the mother of Jesus. Ladies, she rode a donkey while nearing labor.

She RODE A DONKEY while nearing LABOR.

She'd likely been teased and ostracized from her community, after she was terrified by an angel visit that shook her life and filled her soul.

And when the time came to give birth to this Baby, no doulas assisted, and no nurses fussed. Only her new husband was leaned on as he filled the roles of doctor, coach, and father. No onesies or tiny diapers were available; rather, simple strips of cloth from who knows where. No nursery to send Jesus to so she could rest; just the baleful eyes of donkeys and sheep.

Mary probably cried. I hope Mary let herself cry. And then I hope Mary let herself laugh till she cried again at the sheer bizarre and beautiful wonder of it all – the coming shepherds, the life her Son would live, the angel chorus making the night sky brilliant, a braying donkey the soundtrack, her new husband by her side, and a Babe. Her sweet baby boy, born to make her a mama and to make us whole.

And then Mary praised the One who orchestrated it all.

I often think about Mary, mother of Jesus, at this time of year. Mary's home wasn't decorated. Her halls weren't decked. Her burlap centerpiece lay in a manger – a feeding trough for animals – and her baby slept in its hold. Immanuel, God with us, delivered by a teenage couple in a stable.

It was not a perfect and beautiful scene. Weddings weren't held in that barn; it had never seen a tealight candle or a mason jar.

But what it did see, what it did hold, was pure love.

Christmas gives us an opportunity to scrap expectations. The way Christ entered our world was so perfectly imperfect, full to bursting with love and joy, rough around the edges, and so very simple in its appearance. What if we embraced those standards – imperfection, love, joy, simplicity – amidst our to-do tasks and busy season?

Mary didn't expect to become pregnant before she was married. She didn't expect to carry the Savior of the world. She didn't expect to celebrate that first Christmas at all, much less in a borrowed stable.

Yet look at the wonder she welcomed when she threw out her expectations. We can do the same, me and you.

This year, season, week – let good enough truly be enough. Release your heart from the prison of expectations, embrace the hallmarks of that first Christmas (imperfection, love, joy, simplicity), and it just may be your sweetest Christmas yet.

Pray

Lord, we praise You. Right here, right now, I lift my heart in praise to You. This busy, messy, wonderful season is all about and for You. You deserve all of our wholehearted praise, and right here, right now, You have mine. May my expectations fly out the window, and may my heart be open to Your leading. Amen.

Ponder

Right in the midst of your chaos, how are you praising the One who orchestrates your all? In what ways can you release yourself from lofty expectations, and embrace whatever God has for you this season?

Take a Moment

If you don't already have one, Advent calendars are a great way to teach kids about waiting as they count down the days left until Christmas. While there are many varieties of Advent countdowns, our favorites include the classic cardboard boxes with chocolate behind each window, the Melissa and Doug Countdown to Christmas Wooden Advent Calendar, and large coloring pads from the Target dollar section (each day has a new page of activities to color).

ACKNOWLEDGEMENTS

This book was a dream of my heart, and I'm deeply grateful for those who made the space for me to write it.

To those who did the behind-the-scenes tech work, I could not be more impressed by your skill:

Jennifer Tucker, you so beautifully captured the "picture in my head" by designing the most perfect cover art.

Peggy and Mary, editors extraordinaire, you're both wonderfully talented. Thank you for correcting my errors while seeing my heart behind each apostrophe disaster.

To my family:

Mormor, thank you for the childcare, and for being my cheerleader since day one. You're the best and I love you.

Sam, Josie, and Clara: thank you for cheering me on! I'm still not tired of writing. Thanks for decking the halls of my desk with every piece of fall décor we own, and for celebrating with me at the finish line. Theo - welcome to the world, little exclamation point baby. We are so happy to have another reason to celebrate this season. You kids are the reason autumn is so fun!

Jared: thank you for leading the way. For dreaming big with me (and sometimes for me). For formatting and updating, designing and editing. I could not do this – any of this – without you.

And to the One who created autumn: You are glorious, creative, and fun. Thank You for letting Your grand paintbrush run wild during these beautiful, color-drenched months. You are the Originator of beauty. To me, the splendor of Your heart is never more evident than it is during autumn. Thank You for this season, and thank You for the words. Both are like the whipped cream on top of an already fabulous pumpkin spice latte, and evidence of Your great love and grace.

Anna

ABOUT THE AUTHOR

Anna E. Rendell is the author of several devotionals for women and moms, and she also works as a Content Marketing Manager at DaySpring. She is also a speaker who loves sharing encouragement with moms and women. Anna lives in Minnesota with her husband and their four kids, who provide plenty of fodder for her #realmomconfessions online. She loves a good book and a great pumpkin spice latte.

For more from Anna, visit AnnaRendell.com, and find her on all social media as @annaerendell.

MORE BOOKS BY ANNA E. RENDELL

A Moment of Christmas: 25 December Devotions for Moms
This paperback book is for the woman who longs for a season that is intentional and full of joy. Including 25 devotions, plus prayers, recipes, time-tested tips and more! As you prepare your heart for Christmas by reading through these pages, you'll be inspired to drop the pursuit of perfection and chase holy instead. Find *A Moment of Christmas* on Amazon and at annarendell.com/amomentofchristmasbook.

A Moment of Quiet: 25 Two-Minute Prayers for Moms
Each prayer in this e-book is written in the first person so that you may simply sit, breathe, and pray as needed. Pull up a prayer on your phone while you're hiding in the bathroom. Whisper one between laundry cycles. Say another out loud while you're parked in the driveway, not yet ready to go inside. Say a prayer for yourself, and whisper one on behalf of another mother who could use even a moment of quiet. Find this e-book on Amazon and at annarendell.com/quietmoment.

Made in the USA
Coppell, TX
24 October 2023